The Whimsical World of Colin Carr

The Whimsical World of Colin Carr

First published on St. George's Day, April 23rd, 2003, by This England Books, Alma House, 73 Rodney Road, Cheltenham, Gloucestershire, GL50 1HT.

©This England International Ltd., 2003.

Printed in Great Britain by Polestar Wheatons Ltd., Exeter, Devon.

ISBN 0 906324 47 5

6

Contents

Colin Carr the artist who became a Lincolnshire legend

An appreciation of his life and work, compiled by Roy Faiers (Editor of *This England*)

(1929-2002)

Writing a mini-biography of our art editor, the late Colin Carr, is a difficult task — even he would have described it as like trying to nail jelly on a wall! For Colin was no ordinary man, as anyone who knew him would agree. But then, no ordinary man could have produced the kind of whimsical but telling paintings that he became renowned for throughout his adult life. And how fortunate that, before his sad demise in September 2002, he left a treasure trove of more than a thousand pieces of artwork in *This England's* archives. You will find over a hundred of them in this book which we are publishing as a tribute to a rare and outstanding artist whose gifted productions, combining light-hearted humour with deep-rooted nostalgia, will bring many a chuckle and untold delight to countless people for generations to come. That is perhaps a more fitting memorial to his talents than any words of mine. But if there's such a thing as a sense of humour in heaven, I reckon there's one newcomer up there who will be quietly tittering with mirth as I struggle to find the words to describe his life on earth.

Essentially, Colin was a small-town Englishman, a gentle-mannered traditionalist who rarely journeyed far from his home county of Lincolnshire. He was the youngest of seven children — four girls and three boys — born to Magnus John Carr (1890-1975) who hailed from Gateshead (County Durham) and his wife Catherine (1893-1951) who came from Yarm in the North Riding of Yorkshire. At the outset of the First World War, Magnus joined the Royal Lincolnshire Regiment — known as the "Yellow Bellies", due to the bright custard-coloured waistcoats they wore — and fought with distinction in the ferocious battle at Arras, northern France, in 1917. But tragedy was soon to strike the Carr family back home in Gateshead. The first pair of the couple's children — May, then aged four, and Catherine, just two — died after being struck down with "Spanish Flu"

Colin Carr

when the fatal epidemic swept through the whole of Britain and much of the Continent towards the end of the war. Fortunately their only remaining child, Doreen, then just a few months old, did not catch the disease and following his discharge from the army Magnus decided to move his depleted family south to Lincolnshire where he soon got himself a job on the prospering fish docks at Grimsby. That's where the remaining four Carr children were born — Lilian (1920), Jack (1922), Gordon (1925), and finally Colin on August 15th, 1929.

During the Thirties the Carr family lived in a council house at Nunsthorpe, a suburb on the south-western fringe of Grimsby, and Colin often recounted the story of how he and his brother Gordon would look out of the back window of their modest home soon after dawn on Christmas Day waiting for the very moment when the two boys in a family living opposite them switched on their bedroom light, which meant they were now wide awake and would soon be opening their presents. This was taken as the starting signal for Colin and his brother to immediately leap out of bed and begin opening their own Christmas gifts from Santa.

Colin and I would often have a giggle over this old memory we shared — because the two youngsters living opposite were me and my brother, Phil! Hence, we grew up together, lived only a few yards apart, went to the same school, played games with each other in the rural safety of uncluttered streets outside, until the war burst upon us all and changed our childhood idyll forever.

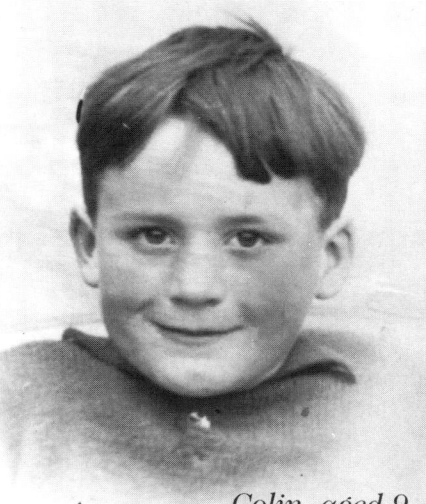

Colin, aged 9

10

This colourful picture aptly portrays the sort of Christmas scene that was commonplace in Colin's pre-war childhood ... a barefoot boy in his pyjamas gazing wistfully at a blazing fire in the living room of his cottage home on Christmas Eve, wondering what gifts from Santa he might find tomorrow morning tucked inside the little stocking seen hanging from the mantel piece. His dutiful mother sits quietly by, cuddling the family cat on her lap while holding a mug of warm cocoa for her little lad before he goes off to bed at a later than usual hour. It is a scene so typical of our innocent English yesterdays, yet now so rare, if indeed it still exists anywhere at all in this ever-changing, television-dominated and increasingly vulgar world.

(continued overleaf)

Colin Carr

Colin attended the local elementary school only a matter of yards from his home, and his artistic prowess quickly began to show itself and earn the notice of his teachers. When he was 12 he won a scholarship to the local Art School in Silver Street, Grimsby, where he studied under the direction of the talented principal, Albert Wade, who was later to remark that Colin, though then still in his early teens, had "got something that I was never blessed with". A prescient compliment indeed, for that inner something was later to blossom out in a variety of ways to the delight of an ever-widening audience of old-fashioned art lovers, including Her Majesty the Queen and her illustrious mother, both of whom placed Colin Carr originals in their collections.

Colin Carr

Back in the Thirties, life for the Carr family in Lincolnshire was still full of traumas. When the Second World War broke out, Colin's father — like many mature men at the time who were considered over-age for active service in the armed forces — volunteered as an Air Raid Warden, assuming duties which were largely in addition to his daily job on the town's fish docks. Two years later their daughter Lilian died of a heart complaint, aged 21. The distraught parents then decided to move their family out of the Nunsthorpe council estate and into a private semi-detached house a few hundred yards away

in nearby Gloucester Avenue, a smarter part of the neighbourhood. But bad luck followed them yet again, for within a few months of settling into their new abode the Germans chose Grimsby as the target for one of their most cunning and devastating bombing raids of the war.

On the night of June 13th, 1943, the Luftwaffe attacked the fishing port with a new terror weapon which had never been used against Britain before — the "Butterfly" bomb.

(continued overleaf)

13

△ An unexploded "butterfly bomb" seen on a railway line at Grimsby in June 1943.

Sized only slightly bigger than an ordinary tin of baked beans, the device had a pair of metal "wings" that opened out when dropped from the aircraft and these helped to slow its descent down to earth, where it was designed to land without exploding. In little over an hour more than 3,000 of these previously unknown but deadly "booby traps" were dropped on various residential parts of Grimsby, with Nunsthorpe bearing the brunt.

They lodged in trees, roof gutters, and lay hidden among flower beds, cemetery graves, vegetable patches and lawns all around the town. Not until the next day did local people begin to discover the full treachery behind this new anti-personnel weapon, when unsuspecting children picked them up in the street or tried to kick what they thought was an empty tin on the pavement, and were blown to smithereens.

14

Colin Carr

As a result, some 99 people, many of them school-children, were killed in Grimsby over the following few days, including old Mr Wilkinson who ran the little corner sweet shop in Nunsthorpe where Colin and I, plus all the other youngsters in the neighbourhood, used to buy our liquorice all-sorts and penny bars of chocolate on the way to school.

As a further piece of trickery on that fateful night, the German raiders also dropped a series of high-explosive bombs to divert attention away from the hidden menace of the "Butterfly Blitz", which was the real reason for the raid. One large bomb fell in the road right outside the Carr family's new home, blasting out a huge crater and causing the front of their house to partially collapse.

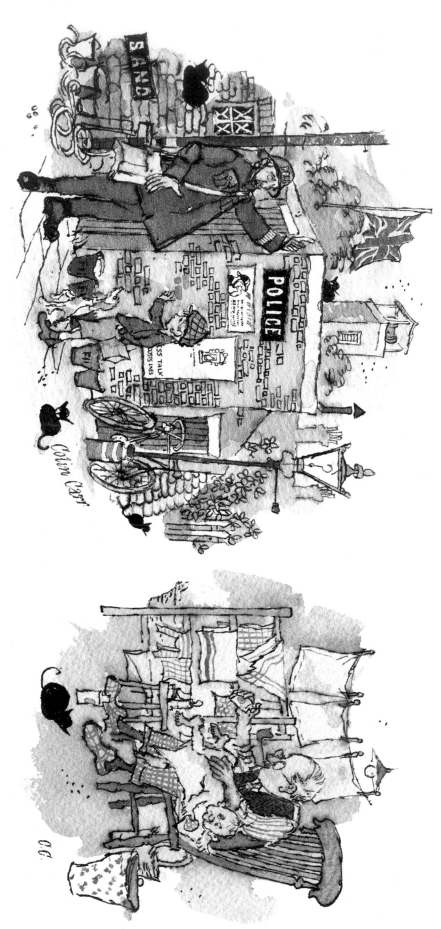

In the front bedroom of the crumpled building, Doreen's baby daughter Valerie Anne, then aged just four months, was trapped in her cot when a slab of masonry fell across it. By the time the family had managed to crawl outside it was feared that the little child had been killed, but Colin — then aged 14 — dashed inside the house with his brother Gordon and, without a moment's hesitation, climbed up the shattered staircase and managed to extricate the baby from her cot and carry her out to safety ... to the joy of her mother and everyone waiting anxiously in the street.

However, due to its serious structural damage, the house was uninhabitable and this meant the family had to move yet again and go back onto the council estate for almost another year until their home was re-built.

Meanwhile, despite the continuing perils of wartime, Colin carried on studying at the local Art School until beginning his National Service in 1947 at the age of 18.

He joined the Royal Air Force and, since there was no obvious use for illustrative artists in the service, he was given training in the dental section and posted to RAF Innsworth near Gloucester — the furthest he had ever

16

travelled away from his Lincolnshire home up to that time.

Despite the seemingly serious side to his new occupation as a dental assistant, Colin continued to develop an impish sense of humour which became a feature of his later life, as testified by many of his friends and reflected by the whimsical characters in hundreds of his paintings.

One instance of this occurred at the RAF base when his company flight sergeant, a particularly ferocious type, arrived at the dental surgery for an appointment. Failing to recognize Colin who, like the dentist himself, was clad in a long medical cloak and wearing a face mask plus a

17

The Company Sergeant Major.

head-cap, the sergeant mistook him for a superior officer and gave him a full miltary salute as he entered the room! Not till the hapless fellow's treatment in the dental chair was over and he was about to depart did Colin slowly slide the mask down from his face to reveal his subordinate identity with a rascally grin, much to the fury of the sergeant … and howls of delight from all the squaddies in the barracks who heard about it later!

After completing his National Service in 1949 Colin returned to Art School at Grimsby and there met fellow student Theodora Sigley who was also a budding artist, though possessing a more conventional style of portraiture. They were married in 1952 and had two sons — Colin John (born 1953) and Christopher (born 1960) — both of whom have inherited a variety of artistic talents from both of their parents.

(continued overleaf)

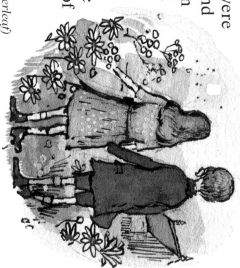

18

△ *The first train to link the East and West coast of England, operated by the Manchester, Sheffield and Lincolnshire Railway company, comes chugging into Grimsby in 1848, as imagined by Colin Carr to mark the line's 150th anniversary in 1998.*

At the outset of his commercial life Colin had gained a position as an office worker and part-time artist in the advertising department of the Humber Graving Dock, a local shipbuilding and repairing company, but he soon moved over to take up a similar position with one of Britain's biggest trawler-owning and fish merchanting companies — the Ross Group. It was while working in their design department on Grimsby's fish docks in the summer of 1965 that his unstoppable, devilish sense of fun rebounded harshly upon him.

The company's founder and chairman, J. Carl Ross, was a well-known captain of industry, and tipped as a likely candidate for a knighthood at the time. He was frequently being pictured in the financial pages of the national Press, and as a bit of fun, just for other members of the staff to see and have a chuckle, Colin got hold of one of the black-and-white photo-prints of his boss and decided to embellish it a little. He drew a make-believe Salvation Army officer's cap on the chairman's head, twisting the peak to one side — "on the slosh", or skew-whiff as it's called in Lincolnshire — so that the big chief looked more like a dippy character portrayed by comedian Charlie Chaplin than a top-ranking leader of industry.

◁ Colin's rather impish
embellishment of a
recent Editor's Letter!

20

But questions were inevitably asked: What was the reason behind the sudden appearance of black cats in his paintings? And why were they almost always depicted as being startled and arch-backed, as though they'd just seen a ghost?

The answer is intriguing, but rather sad.

In the late Sixties, Colin and his first wife, Theo, plus their two sons and a lovely black pussy-cat, lived in a single-storey wooden house tucked down a short and very narrow single-track lane in the Grimsby suburb of Scarthoe. Opposite them, in a similar style house, lived a man who was the instructor at a local motoring school. Every night when he returned home from a full day of teaching learners to drive, he parked his L-plate car in the quiet cul-de-sac, for the houses didn't have room for a garage or driveway.

Having been in constant use throughout the day, the L-car's engine was always hot when it arrived back in the evening, and Colin's pussy eagerly looked forward to its regular return. Choosing the right moment when the coast was clear, it would spring up onto the warm bonnet of the car and snuggle down for an hour or two of comforting sleep ... much to the annoyance of Mr Motorman. He reckoned that little Tiddles left dirty paw-marks on the paintwork of his car, which he needed to keep in pristine condition for the benefit of his business, and his pupils. So he would often pop out of his house and into the lane during the dark hours to creep up on the sleeping cat and shoo it away with a sudden yelp. However, although she beat a hasty retreat, it wasn't long before Tiddles came quietly tip-toeing

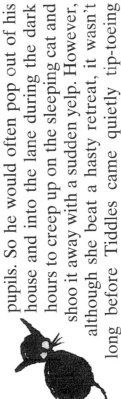

32

back again to leap onto the car bonnet for a further hour or two of quiet snoozing.

This charade went on for many months, causing heated arguments between Colin and his neighbour, until one fateful night. A member of the driving instructor's family worked at a local chemist's shop, and one winter's evening, just before Tiddles had time to leap onto the car as usual, the young fellow placed a plastic saucer on the bonnet containing a deadly poison. Later that night Colin noticed the cat leaping around the garden in a frenzied fit, but after a few more agonising minutes, and a final pitiful "miaouw", it collapsed and died. Colin was deeply upset, but it was not until a few days later that he eventually learned the truth from the local Vet of just what had caused his cat to die in such a horrible way. He was devastated and decided there and then to move to another house half a mile away.

As it happens, while the trauma over his much-loved pussy was going on, Colin was busily trying to finish a painting he had been commissioned to produce by a well-known local fish merchant (see opposite page). The picture was of the Royal Lincolnshire Regiment's military band marching through the centre of Grimsby's Old Market Place, watched by crowds of local onlookers. With poor little Tiddles on his mind so much, Colin decided there and then to give it a touch of immortality, and so he included a small picture of the cat trotting brightly in front of the marching troops! No-one realised its significance at the time, but from then on Colin began including cats in most of his paintings, and it was not until many years later that he revealed to me the original reason for doing so.

(continued overleaf)

33

Colin's life always revolved around the values and emblems of yesteryear. That is to say, in the parlance of the time, he was not "with it". Although he did eventually learn to drive a car, he rarely practised doing so and it was his schoolteacher wife, Ollie (see his painting of her on Page 25), who drove him wherever he wanted to go, mainly weekend jaunts to outlying towns and villages in rural Lincolnshire.

Market places, and the country characters who once frequented them, were his particular favourites, as evidenced by the number he depicted over the years.

As the world of technology went racing ahead towards the end of the century, Colin turned a blind eye to it. He did reluctantly buy a television set, but still preferred listening to the "wireless". Instead of possessing a mobile phone and surfing the Internet on a personal computer,

35

he collected all sorts of minor antiques and bric-a-brac, surrounding himself with the memorabilia of a bygone England. Proof of the inspiration this gave him can be found in the little touches added to many of his pictures — famous old paintings like "Bubbles" and "The Laughing Cavalier" are framed on the walls of his cottage interiors; an old-fashioned rolling pin inscribed with the wifely words "Remember Me" hangs from the mantelpiece; a pair of King Charles spaniels, in pottery form, perch haughtily on the shelf above; and there's invariably a paraffin lamp flickering inside a bulbous globe to bring a golden touch to the cosy scene.

36

Colin's external pictures also followed the pattern of his nostalgic mind. Look at his market place scenes and you will find at least one of the chimney pots has a sweep's circular brush poking out towards the sky. Churches almost always have the Cross of St. George flying aloft from the tower, and Union Jacks abound all over the place, thus displaying the true love of country that Colin felt deeply.

In his pictures of people in the streets, ladies are unfailingly seen dressed in full-length skirts, and both they and their gentlemen escorts always wore hats.

(continued overleaf)

37

Washing lines either have a pair of Grandpa's long-johns or Grandma's long-legged bloomers hanging out to dry. Dogs and foxes can be seen scampering across the road with a string of sausages in their mouths, followed by an irate butcher chasing after them with a cleaver. And there are umpteen startled cats to be seen everywhere. His human characters were equally distinctive — from grey-haired village shopkeepers and flat-capped newspaper sellers to the haughty-looking local Squire and bulbous Bobbies on the beat.

(continued overleaf)

39

Colin loved everything that was traditional about England, including deep red pillar boxes and the welcome sight of a uniformed village Postman on his bike. As a result, his many paintings have provided us with a legacy of English life that was once so very familiar to our parents, but is now fast disappearing into the sludge of history.

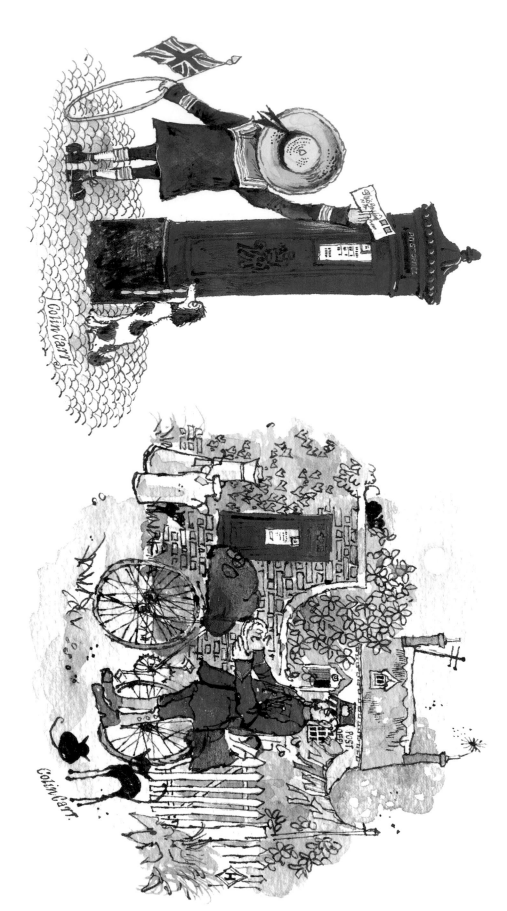

However, Colin's talents were not just confined solely to artwork, for he had a strong literary side as well — including poetry. Later in this volume you will find an interesting story he wrote on travelling through rural Lincolnshire in a country bus, plus an amusing piece of rhyming verse on spending a day at the County Show.

(continued overleaf)

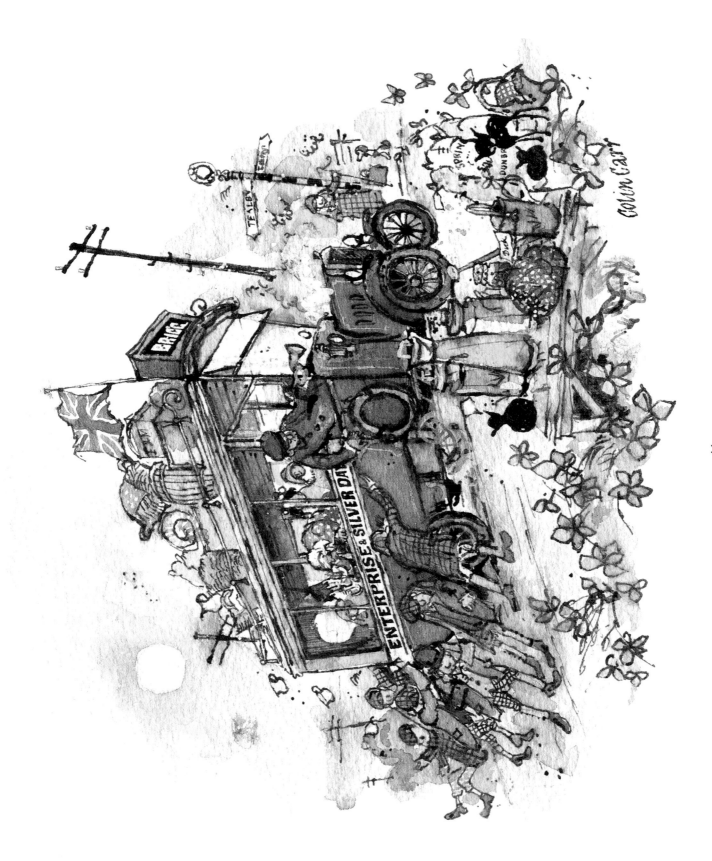

Colin Carr

41

'Cash this please'

Colin Carr

Apart from his love of cats, Colin also had a great affection for foxes and enjoyed their devilish cunning in evading the efforts of the local hunt. Look closely at this colourful scene of huntsmen gathering in the country-

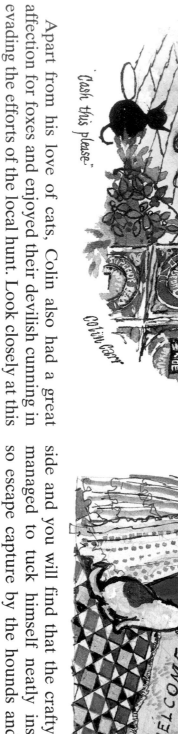

side and you will find that the crafty old Reynard has managed to tuck himself neatly inside a hedge and so escape capture by the hounds and their red-coated masters (see opposite page, bottom right).

43

Colin's idea of going away for a holiday in the summer didn't mean jetting out to some foreign hot-spot. He much preferred the simple pleasures of life walking along the coastal paths of Norfolk, or sitting on the sands at Southwold in Suffolk struggling to do *The Daily Telegraph* crossword. In fact it was while on a short holi-

day at Happisburgh (Norfolk) with his wife and children in the late Sixties that he nearly lost his life. Colin had never learned to swim but he enjoyed taking a dip in the sea. So instead of practising the crawl or the breast-stroke he used to wade slowly out into the tide until the level was somewhere around his midriff.

Colin Carr

(continued overleaf)

44

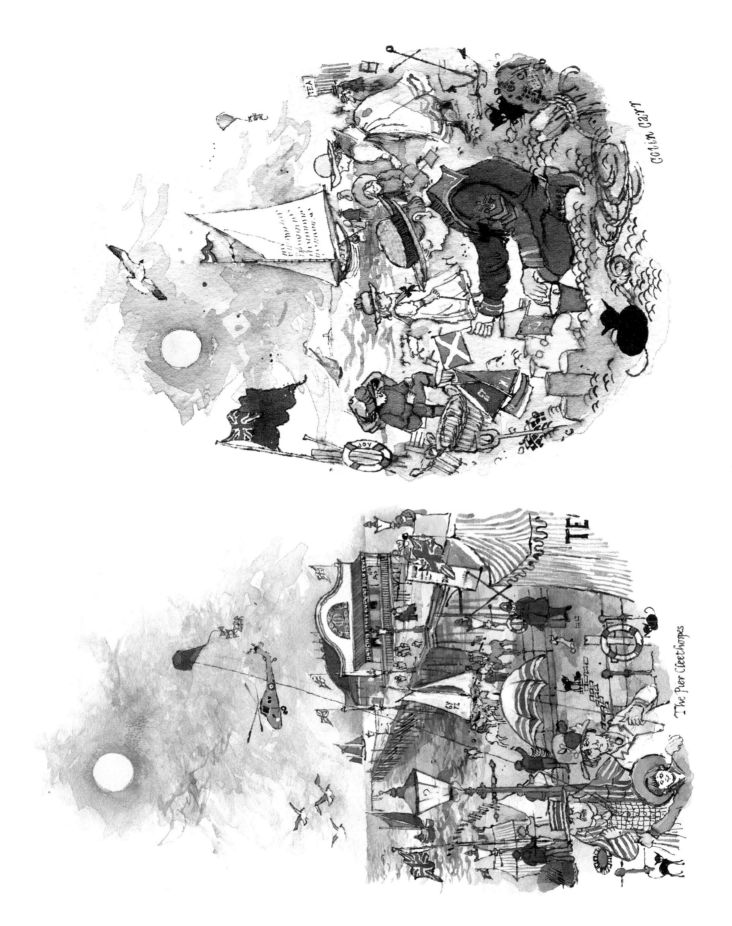

Colin Carr

The Pier Cleethorpes

45

He would then begin jumping up and down, enjoying the rare exhilaration of the North Sea's cold and salty waters splashing all over him.

Watching his antics from the shore was Mrs Eileen Wallis, a friend of the family, who also came from Grimsby and was on holiday down there with her teenage daughter, Helen, a strong swimmer.

On this summer's day the tide was slowly drifting out and the wind was blowing off-shore. Eileen noticed that both of these factors, together with Colin's constant jumping, was gradually taking him further and further away from the beach. Suddenly she saw him stumble and plunge beneath the waves some 50 yards out to sea. As he didn't surface, she shrieked out in alarm for her daughter to come and help her as she dashed into the water

towards the spot where Colin had gone down. Helen, who had already received instruction in life-saving, streaked past her mother and reached the stricken fellow first. Together, one pulling from the front and the

46

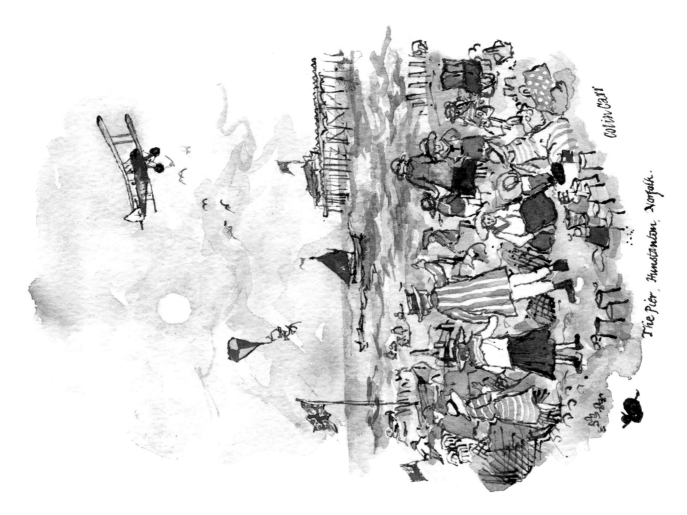

Colin Carr

The Pier, Hunstanton, Norfolk.

other pushing from the rear, they managed to slowly drag him out of deep water until they reached the shallows where he was able to stand up. They then led him back onto the beach where he collapsed on the sands, gasping for a while before fully recovering. It was a close call indeed, and one which Colin never forgot, or failed to be thankful for, all through his life.

C.C.

We hear you went to the theatre recently . . . . .

. . . in a rather revealing gown . . .

Colin's bubbling sense of fun even survived and prospered through the traumas of several surgical operations around the time of his seventieth birthday in the summer of 1999. After our editorial team had sent him a perky "Get well soon" card, including a light-hearted illustration by another member of our art staff (see above),

Colin responded magnificently with this humorous painting (see opposite page) of himself being pushed along in his three-wheeled bath chair propelled by a nurse, accompanied by a pair of dogs scampering along with strings of sausages — and the inevitable black cats.

(continued overleaf)

48

To my dear friends at This England & Evergreen —

Dear All

Thank you from the bottom of my heart for the really wonderful, humorous, witty, clever card sent to me in hospital after my recent operation, and thank you dear Christine for yours - as usual - lovely art work - a masterpiece! In fact my entrance to the operating theatre would have been most spectacular, because I put the gown on back to front! fortunately this was spotted in time - thus saving the theatre sisters' blushes.

I am now able to go in my bath chair on one or two outings in the country and I am beginning to eat a little - today I had the pobs - a wonderful treat!

I enclose a small illustration showing me & my outings with Nurse Blagdon - love to all and one again many thanks to all. Yours ever,

Colin

Colin Carr

ART RAIDERS TAKE £3,000 ORIGINALS

RAIDERS at a Cleethorpes art shop stole pictures worth more than £3,000.

The haul, from S & A Frames in Humber Street, included five Colin Carr originals worth up to

Policemen always figured largely in Colin's paintings and he counted many of the Lincolnshire constabulary among his friends. So it was with some shock in September 1994 that he read in the local newspaper (*Grimsby Telegraph*) that police were investigating a daring robbery at nearby Cleethorpes in which thieves had broken into an art framer's shop and stolen five of his original paintings, today worth several thousand pounds. Even though almost ten years have now elapsed since the theft, the pictures have still not been recovered and the shop's owner, Mr. Rolf Sperr, maintains that they were stolen to order since very few of Colin's original paintings have ever been made available to the public.

Police kept a close eye on art dealers and shops for some time afterwards, but to no avail. Colin's reaction at the time, however, was a mixture of disbelief and humour. For he thought the thieves must have quickly realised their mistake in stealing his paintings, and he suggested the police keep an eye on local "car boot sales" instead! Indeed, within a couple of days of the robbery, he produced this painting (see opposite page) and presented it as a goodwill gesture to the unfortunate art-shop owner, with one distinctive but humorous spelling change. For it says "Carr" boot sale, and values the missing originals at just £6 the lot!

(continued overleaf)

"Colin Carr Originals... Six Quid, the lot!"

△ Colin pictured working at his desk in This England's editorial office at Cheltenham. Below: Colin joins the Editor and his wife, Dorothy, at a reception to mark their Golden Wedding in July 1998. All three were childhood neighbours at Grimsby in the Thirties.

△ Her Majesty the Queen Mother smiles as she is presented with Colin's picture of Happisburgh Lighthouse while on a special flying visit there in July 1990 (see opposite page). Below: Colin and his wife Ollie pictured at a surprise party in Guernsey for his 65th birthday.

Colin Carr

In 1998 *This England* highlighted a major campaign by residents of Happisburgh in Norfolk to save their historic lighthouse from closure following a decision by Trinity House, which administers Britain's lighthouses, to shut it down and sell it on the open market.

Colin Carr illustrated the article in our magazine with this bleak wintry scene, and readers were invited to provide moral and financial support. After a long struggle, Parliament passed a Bill putting the lighthouse under the control of Happisburgh residents, and on 20th July, 1990, just two weeks before her 90th birthday, the Queen Mother flew by helicopter from Sandringham to Happisburgh to congratulate the local people on their victory and, as pictured opposite, to receive Colin Carr's watercolour painting of the lighthouse from Mrs. Christine Payne, Secretary to the Happisburgh Lighthouse Trust.

There was, however, one subtle difference to the picture which appeared in the magazine, for Colin had added a milestone which read "Sandringham 48 miles" — the distance from Happisburgh to the Royal residence in Norfolk!

(continued overleaf)

53

△ Colin produced the cover paintings for several LP records, including these two by The King's Singers, a male close-harmony group whose original six members were choral scholars from King's College, Cambridge. One of the original six, Brian Kay, went on to become a well-known music presenter for BBC radio. (Note the black cat peeping out from below the piano keyboard!)

After a lifetime of friendship, and nigh on forty years as an editorial colleague, Colin Carr — whose wonderful paintings have graced the pages of *This England* since our very first edition in the Spring of 1968 — suffered a series of strokes last year that deprived him of speech, thus sti-fling his chirpy personality and nullifying his devilish sense of fun. He spent the final six months of his life in a nursing home at Bradley, near Grimsby, and while resi-dent there a new conservatory was erected and named after him, as a tribute to Lincolnshire's most noted artist.

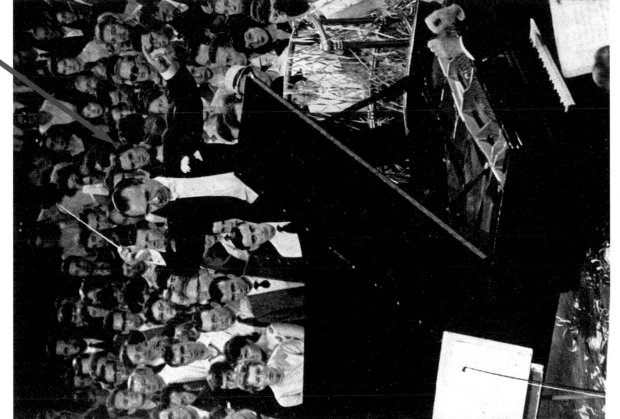

△ *Colin pictured just behind the late Sir Malcolm Sargent seen conducting "The Last Night of the Proms" concert.*

Indeed there may well come a time soon when Colin Carr's paintings are regarded as icons of life in bygone Lincolnshire, in much the same way as the Salford and Manchester areas of Lancashire are identified with the works of L.S. Lowry (1887-1976), creator of the famous "match-stick" men.

Colin departed this life on Saturday, September 14th, 2002, which just so happened to coincide with the annual *"Last Night of the Proms"* concert at the Royal Albert Hall, a famous patriotic event that Colin truly loved all his life (see right).

(continued overleaf)

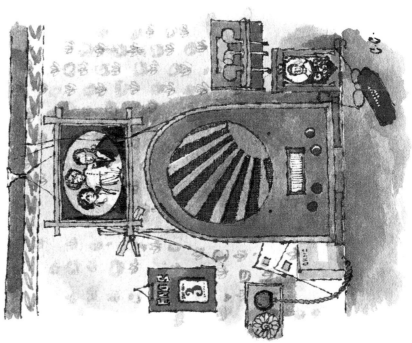

So it was with a heavy heart that I made a nostalgic journey up north to attend his funeral in our home town of Grimsby. Rather than rushing up at breakneck speed along the inter-connecting motorways to attend the very moving service at the parish church only a couple of

hundred yards from his home, which figured in many of his paintings, I spent several hours behind the wheel of a car slowly wiggling my way through the leafy lanes, quiet villages and small towns of rural Lincolnshire which were so close to Colin's heart.

We're off! in a MotorCar!

Colin Carr

(continued overleaf)

56

△ *This classic scene of the market place at Folkingham was presented to the Queen by the Chief Constable of Lincolnshire*

57

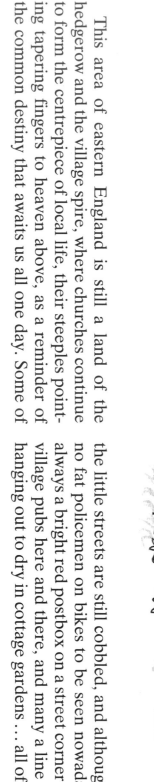

This area of eastern England is still a land of the hedgerow and the village spire, where churches continue to form the centrepiece of local life, their steeples pointing tapering fingers to heaven above, as a reminder of the common destiny that awaits us all one day. Some of the little streets are still cobbled, and although there are no fat policemen on bikes to be seen nowadays, there's always a bright red postbox on a street corner, quaint old village pubs here and there, and many a line of washing hanging out to dry in cottage gardens ... all of which pro-

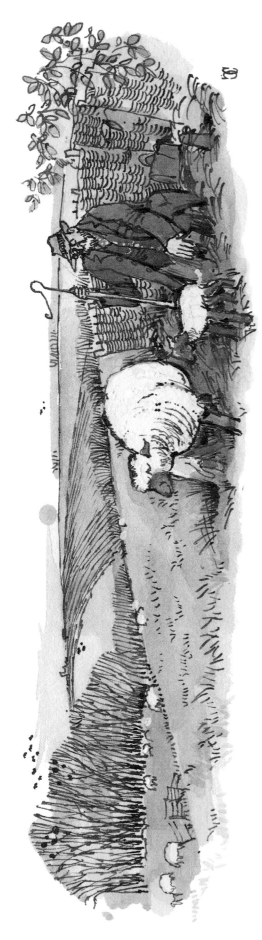

vided inspiration for Colin's uniquely humorous paint-ings, so highly appreciated by all who saw them. No wonder that this part of old England is fast becoming known as "Colin Carr Country", for framed prints of his work can be found in hundreds of homes all over Lincolnshire and — as testified by the Rector of his local church in a funeral address, published within this volume — even old Christmas cards featuring Colin's paintings

Colin Carr

△One of Colin's well-loved Christmas cards, often found framed in homes all over Lincolnshire.

are rarely thrown away. Instead they are often framed or pinned onto walls to provide a year-round smile and also to remind people of a simpler mode of living which is fast disappearing forever.

Had he been a celebrity or a self-publicist and made his mark in the mind-numbing field of pop music, or become either a compliant politician or a shadowy figure in big business, Colin would have been recognised with a mention in the annual Honours List. And yet, knowing him, he would have been extremely reluctant to accept a "gong" for practising the humorous skill that fate had kindly bestowed upon him.

Colin Carr

"The Whimsical World of Colin Carr" is published as a lasting memorial to the unusual but highly-admired talents of a remarkable yet very self-effacing man who never sought to promote himself despite earning the plaudits of fellow artists and the affection of *This England's* two million readers all over the world. So prolific was his artistic output for us over the past 35 years that new and unseen examples of his work will continue to feature in the pages of our magazine for ages to come.

Colin's paintings are much more than colourful and humorous glimpses of the England of yesteryear. They are an artistic commentary on the gradual passing of a wonderful era in our country's rural history, and a warning that despite the continuing and aggressive march of time we must all try to do whatever we can to help preserve our treasured and much-loved English way of life.

For the older you get, the more you realise that it is unique . . . just like Colin Carr.

☐

61

A Day at The COUNTY SHOW

Written and illustrated by Colin Carr

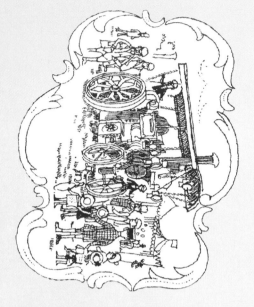

Come Maggie and Bertha, come Sidney and Joe,
We're all ready for the County Show.
The trap is a-waiting and rarin' to go,
Down Rasen Road to the County Show.
The country's blooming, they're scything hay,
The hawthorn is ladened and blossomed with may.
The Cuckoo now singing her one other tune,
Is chased by a Robin from her nest in the broom.
Now Nellie is trotting — the trap's all a-swaying,
Harness bells jingling and brass band a-playing.

The field flitting past us, all haze and hot weather,
And country folk travelling, alone or together,
With horses and waggons as onwards they go,
Down Rasen Road to the County Show.
Now Maggie and Bertha, now Sidney and Joe,
Are excited to get to the County Show.
They argue and sing as they're jogging along,
Past Nettleham Hall and on with the throng
That's wending its way more crowded together,
The Roman Road's endless and gay as the weather.
With Stanhopes and dog carts, a ralli and gig,
As the Nelthorpes speed past in a phaeton from Brigg.
The entrance is nigh — all bunting and banners;
The flags are unfurling and a silver band playing.
Now Maggie and Bertha, Sidney and Joe,
At last have arrived at the County Show.
They tether and water Old Nellie, their mare,
As a steam organ plays all the fun of the fair.
With carousels ridden by folk of North Ormsby,
Past trailers and tractions by Ruston and Hornsby.
The competitors' tent is girded with flowers,
And a shire horse trots be-ribboned and bowered,
Her tail neatly plaited with red, white and blue,
Her brasses all polished and burnished like new.

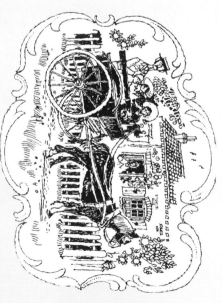

62

Her black gaitered, brown-booted handler so proud,
Is cheered on his way by good friends in the crowd.
To the brass of the band and chug of the tractions,
The friendly "baa" of a Norfolk ewe —
A Percheron mare (foal trotting beside her)
Neighs and whinnies to those she knew.
The distant peels of hunting horns bring,
A parade of the fox-hounds to see,
A high-collared hunting-pinked huntsman so gay,
And a dour-faced Chief Whipper-in.
A military band plays a quickstep by Sousa,
Heralding squadrons of yeomanry proud,
Lances with pennants all fluttering so grandly
Are sure to bring cheers from the crowd.
To flower shows, side-shows, "Aunt Sallys" they went,
And for a pig they bowled.
A soothsayer gypsy in a crystal did gaze,
And their future before them was told.
For Maggie and Bertha and Sydney and Joe,
The time for home-coming is nigh.
The sun whose rays the show had so blessed
Has crimsoned the western sky.
Now Old Nellie, refreshed and ready for home,
Is harnessed and trots on her way.

Her burden is jogged on and into the eve,
As nightingales roundelay.
At last they're home — the oil lamp is lit —
Old Nellie is now in her stable.
The scent of honeysuckle pervades the night,
And their supper is set on the table.
A day to remember was had by all,
Though now it is so long ago.
That glorious day in the month of June
When we all went to the County Show.

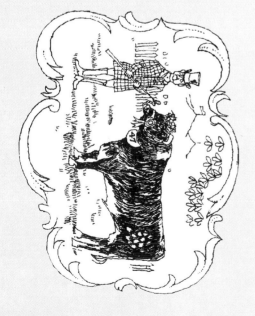

63

The Empty Chair

Often in the soft core of the evening
Before it had deepened
Into the hardness and silence of night,
With its trappings of stars …Moonlight.
We would sit round the fire in the pool of the lamp,
She with her knitting
And I with my pipe and my book,
Reading sometimes a passage aloud
For the pleasure of seeing her eyes grow bright
With that warm and wonderful look of interest shared.

It is hard to remember
The day it all closed like the book
That we finished together.
Hard to remember
When rain became rain again
Tapping on glass,
Not tears on my brain.
Or how the lane became choked with weeds
Where we used to walk in the warm summer twilight.

So long ago since the old copper kettle
Shone bright on the hob,
Or Bob, the mongrel, stopped moaning
And gazing with brown haunted eyes at her empty chair.
Yet, now I am old there are still all the memories.
Days are distilled with them,
Evenings all filled with them,
So much so, I sometimes forget that she's gone …
I imagine I hear her light step on the stair,
Or turning the key in the lock
And look up to greet her,
But seeing the empty chair I remember
The day it all closed like the book
That we finished together…

(Poem by EILEEN WARREN)

64

The Waiting Chair

Old age comes not consciously at first,
For still in the mind
Is mirrored the earnest, decisive young chap
Who wakes each morn to the challenge of a new day.
Whole, unshakeable, perhaps a little dogmatic.
Then creeping in — rather pleasantly —
That little term "Sir"
For men I considered quite elderly!

But small incidents take place
That rankle and rub — allay the young chap's ghost.
Take that day in a pub
Drinking with strangers, two generations between,
With no sense of fun. Unable to laugh
At my good old yarns, but boasting their college debates
As though I had been to no school —
No rigorous Sandhurst — and patronised,
Calling me "Dad" as they would an old fool.

But now I look in the mirror and see
a rather stooping greybeard,
And take care to stick to the old haunts,
The old friends who welcome you,
Keep a waiting chair for you,
Knowing you as you are, and as you have been.

And there comes an acceptance of old age
But more gradual than transition of child to man,
More gentle, and in some ways more enjoyable.
You can say what you want to say
Without fear of causing pain,
You can live brave moments again and again
With pride, and in comfort.
You can make eyes at Rosie the barmaid
Without commitment.

Taken all round it is an age of warmth and pleasure,
Not to be regretted, especially together ... with friends.

(Poem by EILEEN WARREN)

66

67

THE COUNTRY BUS

A ride through rural Lincolnshire, written and illustrated by Colin Carr

Have you ever thought of how much you miss when you travel by car? Of course you get there quicker and it's possibly more comfortable — but if you want a journey in which you see not only the glories of the countryside, but also a microcosm of life in general, then take my advice and go by bus — a country bus, of course; town buses are quite a different kettle of fish.

Firstly, let's take bus conductors, quite a race apart and usually quite brilliant fellows. They always seem to whistle, and at least one of "my" conductors whistles the whole first movement of Rachmaninov's 2nd Piano Concerto (no mean feat on a bus travelling along a bumpy Lincolnshire road).

Then we have the dry-humoured conductor who says a few quiet words in the ear of one of his "regulars" who then goes into fits of laughter and says: *"That's a good 'un Cyril"* — but you can never quite hear what the "good 'un" is!

Kindly-faced old fellows get onto my country bus — old men with flowered scarves tied stock-wise and usually revealing a blue-striped union shirt and a rather large gilt collar-stud. They wear two waistcoats, or one waistcoat and a grey home-knitted cardigan, and always a seasonal flower in the lapel of their conductor Oxford tweed jacket. When asked by the conductor how they

feel today, the inevitable reply is — in a very loud, broad Lincolnshire accent (impossible to write in dialect): *"Not over bad ye knaw, but 'a do get a touch of lumbeägor."*

Before the end of our journey, the old man has gone into details of his past history, of the days when he left Lincolnshire with his pine box of belongings to be a farm labourer on the estate of a now extinct baronet in Wiltshire; details of agricultural shows and far-off harvest suppers, Jubilee celebrations and fox-hunting; of how he came home again to Lincolnshire. A silver "turnip watch" (chain driven) is brought out with great ceremony during our journey and taken out of its case to reveal the inner fretted back plate of great intricacy and beauty. Also taken out about half-a-dozen times is a vast, faded red polka-dotted handkerchief to wipe away the inevitable dewdrop that forms on the end of his finely-chiselled nose.

His pale blue eyes light up at the memory of his wife. *"She's been gone these many a-year — she were a good 'un, aye … aye … aye … she were that."* He lights his pipe, a small, old-fashioned briar, and looks out at the passing fields through misted eyes as we journey onwards — our conductor humming part of Elgar's 'Cello Concerto with great delicacy.

"*All tickets please!*" — it's the ticket inspector! Now I don't know about you, but if there's one thing I don't like it's ticket inspectors. Don't get me wrong — I, of course, have nothing against them personally, but I *lose* tickets. Well not exactly lose, but during the day-dream one inevitably has on a country bus ride, tickets just vanish. You put it safely away one minute, and the next minute — well, you get it out of your pocket, show the inspector, and lo and behold, he gives

The inspector has a few words with the conductor and looks in my direction with a sad shrug of his shoulders and leaves us to go on our way to pick up more passengers. One of them looks like a solicitor's clerk, a tall, grey-haired old man with spectacles and proudly carrying a very fine silver-handled Malacca walking stick. He sits down and announces to the bus that he has retired that very day, and that the walking stick — suitably engraved — was a farewell present from his staff. And from the little admiring glances he gives it, between taking pinches of snuff, a much appreciated one — let us hope it helps him along the remaining road of his retirement!

Now I haven't as yet mentioned what you see out of our bus. If it is a double-decker, I go on the top deck — in this way not only can you admire the countryside in perspective, but you can also see into windows of the houses you pass. I hasten to add that the bus is travelling at about 30 miles an hour, and you can only glance. But a glance is often enough to reveal the true character of a room.

you a charming smile and says, in an unemotional voice: *"This ticket, sir, appears to be a little out of date, sir. Last November, sir."* Well, after a lot of fumbling — with our inspector whistling patiently between his teeth (inspectors *always* whistle between their teeth), standing by and watching you as you go through your pockets, and, *found it!* In a completely different pocket from the one I put it in, but you see, all this is part of the magic of a country bus ride.

A glimpse, for instance, through a Wesley Chapel window, revealing pine box pews and swinging oil lamps, is always a delight. Or the sight of a magnificent old iron bedstead with shining brass knobs; of Minton water jugs and basins on pine wash-stands; of little country-made beech chairs, and in at least one bedroom on our route can be seen a superb patch-work quilt worked in silk, satin and velvet (this, seen through a maze of old decorative net curtains on a large feather-bed, is quite a charming little cameo). Past the almshouse, and take a look at those cast-iron garden seats, standing in front,

shaped like the branches of a tree with snakes intertwined around the legs.

Letter boxes never fail to fascinate me, their scarlet always brightens up any part of the English countryside, and many varieties can be seen from our vantage point — V.R., E.VII.R., G.V.R., G.VI.R., E.II.R. — covering five different reigns. Letter boxes mounted in brick pillars (a yellow elec-tion bill stuck on the side giving a further touch of colour), boxes mounted on the side of telegraph poles, and set into the ivy-covered walls of village post offices.

Now we are going past a small cottage, pantile roof, semi-detached, through whose small windows (and a variety of geraniums and other cottage window plants) could be seen, whatever the season, a glowing fire.

Occasionally one would see an old lady peering out at our bus; but mostly it was just the glowing fire, highlighting the homely bric-a-brac of an old country cottage ... always knowing as we rode by that as long as the fire burns brightly all was well within.

The day came when no fire could be seen. A week or so later, still no fire. Later still, the net curtains had been taken down from the little win-

dow and all was deserted. Alas, the old lady had died. The small garden she had tended, although now overgrown, still contains a variety of spring bulbs and marigolds that glow like a perennial memorial, as the fire once did in the grate of

72

this small Lincolnshire cottage.

Now sitting in front of me is a delightful couple. A lady, I imagine, in her early sixties — and, I should say, in her day rather "flighty". You know the type — frizzy pale ginger hair, rather a large powdery made-up face, and a cigarette drooping from thin, flame-red lips. Her companion whom she surveyed through half-closed eyes, was, on the other hand, a simple, old-fashioned, flat-capped and be-gaitered farmhand carrying a large, supermarket plastic carrier bag. Now, naturally I would never listen to a conversation, but being on our country bus and in such close proximity it was impossible not to overhear their discussion.

"Now, you're sure you want to?" the lady said.

A very quiet Lincolnshire voice answered: "I do, I do, of course I do, of course I do. You know I do."

As you can imagine, I was by now quite intrigued by this conversation, and pretended not to hear, and looked out of the bus window.

"Do you think they'll like me? Do you?... think they'll like me?

You won't regret it — that you won't. I'll see you're all right...

I'll get married in me puce dress — you know, the one I wore at Doll's.

I'll see you're all right for pocket money. You'll be all right — you will."

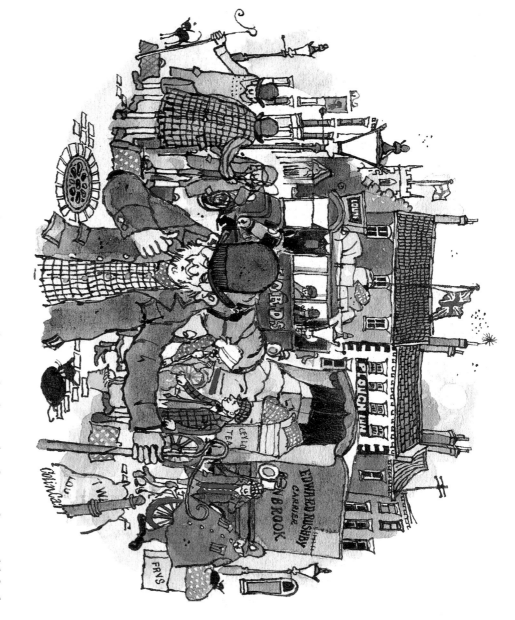

There was a very happy look on the face of our old-fashioned countryman as he offered his betrothed a Nuttall's "Minto" from a crinkly paper bag, which she refused as she lit yet another "Park Drive". Our conductor was now whistling part of the theme song to the film "Limelight" with great gusto as he noisily counted coins and placed them into blue paper bags.

(continued overleaf)

We pass a tiny village butcher's shop with small-gated doorway and catch a glimpse through the windows of brilliantly polished brass scales and weights, of a straw-lined basket of brown and white eggs, pork pies, pork and bacon hocks and chaps, pigs' trotters and poultry, and a blue-striped aproned butcher, smiling as he weighs a pound of tripe for an old-age pensioner. We note the nicely-written sign name over the shop (and we note also that they are "Licensed to deal in game").

As we go on our way I make a point of looking out for the farm wagon in the corner of that field.

You can just see it — a Lincolnshire waggon, but alas quietly decaying away, its Prussian blue paintwork now faded, but still a tribute to the skill of the craftsman who built her 120 summers ago. Lincolnshire is indeed fortunate in having one or two of these elegant waggons carefully preserved. William Morris, once calling something "handsome", added: *"Not the handsomeness of a fashionable dress, but of a farm waggon."* How right he was.

Our country bus drives on, getting cheery waves from an old man with a yoke and two pails, and his wife still wearing an old-fashioned finely-patterned print sun-bonnet — surely

74

a rare sight in Lincolnshire, though I believe more common in parts of Yorkshire.

And there, *quick!* Can you see him? There he goes — all eyes turn to the corner of a small field — a fox, a quick flash of russet and a tip of white ... and gone ... but I always get a thrill to see dear old Reynard. The pageant of the hunting field in all its hunting pink, canary yellow, black and white glory, can never compare with the sheer beauty of that graceful little animal they hunt. My goodness, we're nearly there!

How time flies.

"Market Place ..."

We have now reached our destination — our kindly-faced old man with the flowered scarf (who had dozed off, far away into an Edwardian summer) gives a sudden start, blinks and again takes out his old watch and compares it with the Market Hall clock and mutters, "*Aye, aye, not too bad, not too bad — only three minutes late ...*" his mumblings about carriers' carts are drowned in the general commotion of disembarking passengers. Our newly-retired friend walks proudly away, his hand firmly gripping his new walking stick. Our couple, now arm-in-arm, walk slowly across the Market Square — oblivious to the world.

I sit awhile and admire the architecture of the square. Our conductor whistles "*Pale Hands*" in rather a quavering tone and lifts a folding pushchair down to a waiting mother and child, takes one of those vague, labelled parcels (invariably carried on all country buses) into his arms and looks at me — "*Market Place, sir, we're here.*" I mutter a word of thanks as I slowly

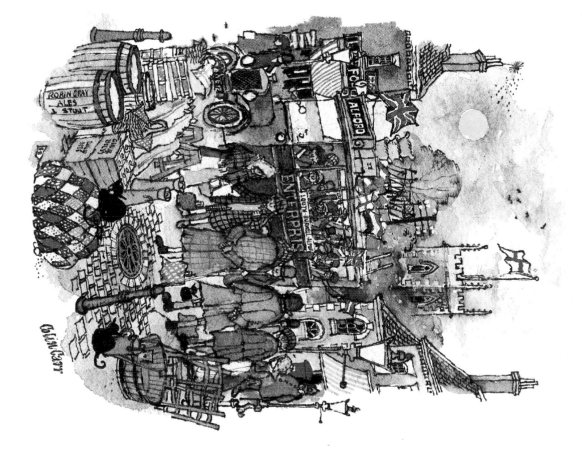

walk down the empty bus. I'm not in a desperate hurry to get anywhere though. I don't even really want to get off. You see, I like country buses so much ... *I only come for the ride!*

The Doctor

Colin Carr has managed to recapture the essential atmosphere of the village doctor's surgery and the old-fashioned chemist's shop on these pages. The doctor occupied the most respected place in the local community, for he was someone you could turn to in time of trouble as well as sickness. He acted as both a friend in need and "father confessor" to rich and poor alike.

In many cases there was no need to hurry into town to have the local chemist make up potions and pills from a prescription he had written down, since most country doctors dispensed their own medicines for the usual run of minor complaints. As a result, like the chemist, he went through life exuding an aroma of menthol tinged with California syrup of figs and senna pods!

Sadly, the medical veterans of those days have long since been buried beneath a mountain of red tape and paperwork due to the ever-increasing bureaucracy of our National Health Service.

The Chemist

Childhood visits to the chemist's shop were always an adventure, for the bespectacled, grey-haired gentleman behind the counter shared a privileged position in society almost on a par with the village doctor, parson and policeman. He was a poor man's physician, always ready to help, advise and, occasionally, diagnose. Some would pull teeth — quickly efficiently and with no anaesthetic — for sixpence!

Customers of all ages were in awe of his neat arrays of coloured glass bottles and pottery jars, ornately lettered in an abbreviated medical Latin which meant nothing to the layman. His batteries of polished wood drawers with their brass handles were equally intriguing.

The shop's wonderful pungency is largely a memory now, and so too are the common remedies without which no household in those days could fight illness and disorder — sweet nitre and tincture of rhubarb, cascara and ipecacuanha.

Some chemists sold spectacles and most had their own specially formulated ointments, cough cures, asthma remedies and liniments — red ochre, sulphur, oils, spirits and varnishes were all part of the stock in trade.

The chemist's shop of today has changed its livery of brass and wood, bright bottles and bawdy smells for a refined, chromium-plated, brightly-lit world of little bottles, myriad pills and tubes of various antiseptic creams.

Its shelves groan with alien commodities undreamed of half a century ago — for the wind of change has blown hard and long through the spice jars and the pill boxes of the traditional chemist's shop.

The Village Squire

Holding an undisputed place in our English country life, the Squire is sometimes a titled landowner, but more frequently a farmer. His home is generally a Georgian country house, built partly as a residence but now forming the headquarters of a farming community. There is a coach house, now used as a garage, lots of stables, barns and granaries, plus a miscellaneous assortment of smaller buildings.

He visits the market in the nearest country town twice a week, using the same inn as his father and grandfather before him. While they travelled the ten miles by using a smart gig and well-groomed mare, our modern Squire drives his own Rover four-wheel drive.

Born and bred in the country, he rarely visits the big city, and on such an occasion, usually his wife's shopping spree, he is glad to get back to his countryside. A regular churchgoer, he plays a prominent part in local affairs and is often a Justice of the Peace and/or Chairman of the Parish Council. His wife is an active worker for the village Women's Institute or the Mothers' Union, and organises the work of the local W.R.V.S.

The Squire is known, like his wife, to everyone in the village, for he is a great believer in the welfare of the local community and gives as much trade as he can to the village craftsmen and local shop-keepers.

He likes to be thought of as a father figure to his farm workers, and while welcoming mechanisation on the farm, he can recall the days when upwards of thirty men were employed on his estate, and when the traditional harvest supper was the highlight of the year. Nowadays he treats his men and their wives to a trip to London for the Smithfield Show and a tour of the shops.

His summer-time sport is cricket. Gone are the days when he could trust his bat and eye as the wagoner's boy hurled down his scorchers. Now the Squire spends most summer Saturday afternoons in one of his own

78

fields, let to the village cricket club for a peppercorn rent, watching the local team perform, from the shade of the pavilion, which his great-grandfather donated to the club many years ago.

The Village Squire still contributes a great deal to the country scene. Despite the many social upheavals of today, let us hope that his kind will survive and prosper in the England of tomorrow.

The Clergyman

Church-going in times gone by was far more popular than it is today, for almost everyone in rural England attended a weekly service at their own denomination's place of worship. The village's Anglican parson, or other local clergyman, was regularly called upon to administer the sacrament of baptism, plus later confirmation, marriage, and eventually a funeral service and burial rites for all local families. In those days it was unheard of for children not to be christened with holy water at the font within a few days of being born, followed some weeks later by the "purification" of the mother in church, thus keeping up with an ancient biblical custom.

There was, of course, no suggestion in that era of women being called to enter the priesthood, although some devout girls — mainly Roman Catholics — joined a nunnery and carried out excellent work as schoolteachers, running orphanages, ministering to elderly people and nursing

the sick. Indeed, in those strict religious days it was considered a near sacrilege for a woman to attend church without wearing a hat or some kind of headpiece. Look around you at a service in your local church these days and you will hardly ever see a lady in a hat, except perhaps when it's a wedding ceremony.

Lincolnshire is often considered to be the birthplace of Methodism, due to the fact that its founder, John Wesley (1703-1791) was born at Epworth, a small market town near Gainsborough, where his father was the rector. John and his brother Charles (1707-1788) went across the Atlantic to Georgia in 1735 to begin converting the Americans to their "born again" philosophy.

The Lacemaker

Lace-making was a cottage industry that spread across England as a result of the influx of migrants from Holland and Belgium during the religious and political persecutions of the Middle Ages. The prime areas where lace-makers settled over here was in the East Midlands — particularly the Nottingham area — and Devon, though in due time it was taken up by local ladies in many parts of Britain in order to augment the meagre incomes of their menfolk.

In the early 1800s special schools were set up where abandoned or orphaned children as young as five — boys and girls alike — were taught pillow lace-making, which involved twisting and plaiting threads and beads wound from a variety of bone and wooden bobbins. Many of these Poor Law institutions were banished in the mid-19th century and pillow lace-making declined as a result, except as a productive side-line for house-bound wives and elderly maidens who became renowned for their skills and the quality of their finished work.

Today, lace-making in England is all but extinct, even as a pastime, due to increasing mechanisation and imports from overseas, notably China and other parts of the Far East.

82

The Tailor

Tailoring is a craft which has been hit hard by the multiple stores and "off-the-peg" buying of clothes. At one time, most villages in the country had their own tailor, and they had enough work to keep them busy all the year round. Nowadays, the customer pays more for a made-to-measure suit or costume, but a century ago everyone was measured for his suit, whether he was rich or poor.

The village tailor was the first to feel the impact of cheap rail fares to the market towns and the cut-price multiple firms. Now, the empty village shop once used by a tailor can frequently be picked out by its large windows, for of all craftsmen the tailor needed plenty of light to ply his craft.

As he sat cross-legged in his window, he saw much of what was going on in the village and he competed with the shoe-maker as a purveyor of local news. His shop was reasonably warm too, for his iron was always heated ready for use. A warm meeting-place was an important point when the village elders met to chat about world problems of the day.

Tailors did much work for the Squire and the landed gentry. They wanted everything to be as near perfect at possible, so it speaks much for their skill that they could fulfil orders for hunting pink, and also livery for the large numbers of servants, whose uniforms were embellished with buttons embossed with the master's family crest.

Other work for the big house included velvet waistcoats for the boys, damask curtains with silk decorations, curtain-holders and bell pulls. Funeral orders, with deep mourning the rule, meant working all night and the tailor's wife would be brought in to help, and also to measure ladies for their costumes. This was perhaps why tailors tended to marry dress-makers — thus keeping their trade "in the family".

83

The Farmhand

Farmers were the main employers in the England of yesteryear, long before the Industrial Revolution took command of the economy by creating factory jobs in towns and cities, thus causing a huge shift of population from the rural peace of the countryside. Most boys left school before they reached their teens and a low-paid job on a nearby farm was often the only task an untrained youngster could take on. Many men decided to remain as farm-workers for the whole of their lives, preferring the peace of a village community to the noisy life of a factory hand in a grimy city back-street.

Ploughing, sowing, reaping and harvesting were the farmhand's way of marking the slow passage of time throughout the year, but he paid a price of virtual poverty for the privilege of working on the land. As a result poaching was commonplace in Victorian England, and indeed it was a virtual necessity to many poor cottagers and farmhands who were badly housed, low paid and under-nourished. Their diet was mainly of root vegetables and bread, with occasional salty, boiled bacon or a pork joint from a friendly farmer. Fresh meat and fish were beyond their purse, and the only hope was for the menfolk to catch a couple of rabbits on a Saturday night, or very early Sunday morning — their only free time from work in the fields. Sometimes a kindly Squire or land-owner would give permission for his workers to catch game on the estate ... but more often than not they employed game-keepers to prevent poaching.

In the 18th-century — when the singing of the traditional old song, printed here, was popular — a law of the time forbade anyone to kill game unless he was related to the Squire. Poaching then became an offence of trespassing upon another's land in pursuit of game, and the penalties were strictly enforced. Although a man found poaching during daylight hours could only be fined for his offence, a man caught at night faced being transported to Australia for seven years!

Colin Carr 76

84

The Poacher

When I was bound apprentice
   in famous Lincolnshire
Full well I served my master,
   for more than seven year,
Till I took up to poaching,
   as you shall quickly hear,
Oh, 'tis my delight on a shiny night
   in the season of the year.

As me and my companions
   were setting of a snare,
'Twas then we spied the game-keeper
   — for him we did not care,
For we can wrestle and fight, my boys,
   and jump o'er anywhere.
Oh, 'tis my delight on a shiny night
   in the season of the year.

As me and my companions
   were setting four or five,
And taking on 'em up again,
   we caught a hare alive,
We took the hare alive, my boys,
   and through the woods did steer,
Oh, 'tis my delight on a shiny night
   in the season of the year.

I threw him on my shoulder,
   and then we all trudged home,
We took him to a neighbour's house,
   and sold him for a crown,
We sold him for a crown, my boys,
   but I did not tell you where,
Oh, 'tis my delight on a shiny night
   in the season of the year.

Success to every gentleman
   that lives in Lincolnshire,
Success to every poacher
   that wants to sell a hare,
Bad luck to every game-keeper
   that will not sell his deer,
Oh, 'tis my delight on a shiny night
   in the season of the year.

85

The Shepherd

Whether he tended his flock roaming across the wide open spaces of the Lincolnshire Wolds, or amidst the grassy slopes of the fertile Cotswolds, the shepherd was always regarded as something of a unique character by his fellow countrymen. For unlike them he spent most of his working day bereft of human company, with only his faithful dog as a friend and willing helper.

In days gone by, most shepherds gave names to each one of their sheep, and it doubtless kept them mentally alert to remember them all in a flock often numbering more than a hundred.

The first lamb born in the initial cold weeks of the year — as pictured in this poignant Colin Carr painting — was always regarded by the shepherd as being rather special, for its survival foretold the likely prospect for the whole of his new flock.

By custom, the shepherd would cuddle the first-born lamb in his wooden hut. By another ancient custom, when the shepherd himself died a lock of lambswool was placed in his hand before the body was buried — as a sign that this new-comer to the pearly gates shared the same calling as his eternal Master above … the Good Shepherd.

The Village Bobby

Of all the characters that flourished in a typical English village, the one person who stood out head and shoulders above all the rest was the policeman — the local "Bobby". By the very nature of his profession, he remained aloof from the usual village activities. He was not encouraged to join in the local social life, for his superiors thought he might favour his friends in some small way if they had been caught breaking the law.

If he were single, and started courting a village girl with a view to matrimony, his senior officers would make discreet enquiries as to her character and suitability to become the wife of a police constable. This practice was rigidly adhered to right up to the Second World War, and there are still some policemen's wives around today who were thoroughly "vetted" before being accepted by the Force.

When the Village Bobby had married, his wife was not allowed to take on any sort of job, full or part time, for again the overwhelming fear of showing favour was always present. The husband likewise was forbidden to do any part-time work for others, and so many of them became keen gardeners and greenhouse specialists, for their shift duties often gave them plenty of daylight hours to use up.

The policeman worked a shift of eight hours, and had various patrol points where the visiting inspector and he himself could meet at certain fixed times. If he had a bicycle, he could have a small allowance for it, and this extended the range of his patrol considerably. The policeman would often wheel his cycle down the village street, but then it must be admitted that the sight of a Bobby walking along the footpath is much more of a deterrent than one policeman cycling by, or flashing past in a police car.

The Village Bobby became known to everybody, but more importantly, he came to know everybody, and he was soon able to weigh up the local trouble-makers. Cheeky or apple-stealing boys would receive an accurately aimed clip on the ear. Can you imagine the result of this immediate punishment in today's politically correct world?

87

The Village Shopkeeper

In today's world of monster supermarkets, persuasive advertising and high pressure salesmanship, the incredible clutter that symbolised the traditional village shop has largely disappeared. The old-fashioned shop scenes depicted here have certainly gone, but the memories they evoke must still be vivid for some whose childhood shopping was a Saturday adventure.

In a sense, the village store was the supermarket of its day. It kept everything; but here the semblance ends, for you just did not serve yourself, or listen to piped music, or pay the girl at the adding machine, or carry ready-made meals home in a small frozen carton.

Shopping at the old village store was quite a warm experience where you received personal attention, advice when sought, a spot of village gossip when available, and a friendliness at most times — particularly if you were not always buying things "on tick"!

The shopkeeper, in company with the vicar, policeman and doctor, was one of the village peers — a father figure, the target of some but the friend of most. Above all he knew his customers, and his wares. We who take frozen foods and pre-packs for granted should try to imagine when tea was scooped loose out of big tins, butter was sold off the slab, and peas, beans and lentils were displayed by the sackful.

Food of every description, and dozens of other domestic items were the stock in trade, for let it not be forgotten that the village shop was the heart of the community. It was vital; it gave credit, it gave service. If it were deficient the community suffered, for telephones and transport were not what they are today. Hot in summer and cold in winter, the old village shop was part of England's pictorial history.

The Little Shops of England

Oh! little shops, Oh! little shops,
They say you've had your day
But I have loved you, little shops,
And I will have my say.

For when we came to visit you,
Within your creaking door
In winter-time, there stood and purred
An oil-stove on the floor,

And by its side, invitingly;
A comfortable chair.
And we could sit and rest awhile,
And round your high shelves stare,

And when we came in summer-time
The door stood open, wide,
And, mingling with malt vinegar
Rose scent blew right inside,

And soap, and string, and lemon curd
Such pretty jumble made;
Brown sugar glistened in a tin —
We loved to watch it weighed.

Dear little shops! You smelt so sweet,
You treated us with care,
You stood and gently talked with us
And gave us such good fare.
You always said. "Good-morning!"
And you said. "Good-afternoon"
And "How is mother then, today?
Hope she'll be better soon."

But now we all stand in a queue
In supermarket blare,
And, crossly waiting, close behind,
Nineteen bold youngsters glare.
We load the steely baskets up,
We place them on the stand,
'Tis sharply, sharply reckoned up,
And banged back in our hand.

Colin Carr

And then we must move on, move on
(There's lots to do today!)
And though our groceries are no more
There's three times as much to pay

And, having paid it, out we go,
(With *"Surprising Offers"* furled)
The sickly music left behind
Into this brash new world.

ALFORD

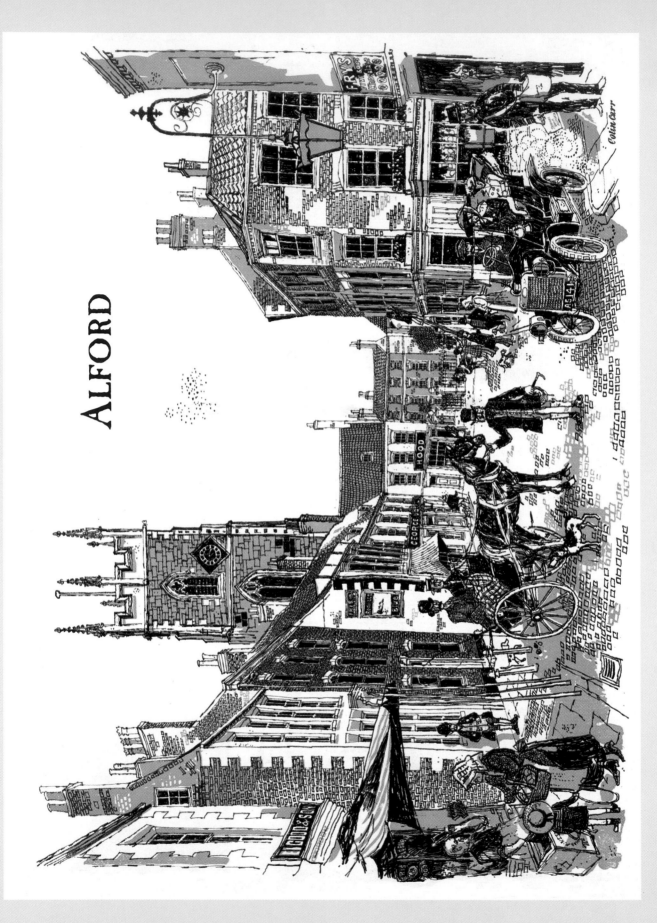

BOSTON

91

SLEAFORD

92

LINCOLN

93

The Little Roads of England

by TEMPLE GRAY

Oh, the little roads of England
They have me in their spell,
They only share their secrets
With those who love them well.
The little roads are gracious,
They have a happy smile,
They give you lasting beauty,
With every twisting mile.

I do not mean the great roads,
The Roman roads, the straight roads,
The Pageantry-of-State roads,
The can't-stop-'cos-I'm-late roads,
That link the crowded towns.
But the little roads, the by-roads,
The jolly little sly roads,
The just-the-you-and-I roads,
The find-us-for-we're-shy roads,
That run below the Downs.

Where'er you go in England
The little roads you'll find,
But only those who love them
Can find there peace of mind.
Their furry folk will greet you,
Their birds sing loud and clear,
And you will hear them always
Till last night's shade draws near.

For I do not mean the fast roads,
The clear-my-way-and blast roads,
The why-must-you-get-past roads,
The no-respect-for-caste roads,
That make this land a hell.
But the little roads, the clear roads,
The bread-and-cheese-and-beer roads,
The come-and-and-love-me-dear roads,
The never-mind-you're-here roads,
That hold me in their spell.

The end of the line...

The line has gone.
They've closed it down.
The gleaming rails have
      turned to brown.
The station's closed,
      deserted, bare.
Decay and rubble everywhere.
Boarded windows, broken glass,
Platform garden choked with grass
And weeds. An air
Of desolation and despair:
No busy, bustling, friendly life
(*"A single, please, Bert.
How's the wife?"*)
No chocolate in the slot machine
(One doubts if there had ever been).
No 4-6-2s. No steam. No smoke.
No slamming doors. No busy folk
To spill from First and Thirds.
No greetings. No waved farewells
or lovers' meetings.
At night no distant whistle blows,
No red or green from oil lamp glows.
No tinkle from the signal box
To say she's passed old Albert Fox
At Copse Hill Junction down the line;
A minute late, but doing fine.
No down, no up. No fast, no slow.
The 10.15 went *years* ago.

(Poem by Sidney W. Budd)

96

Funeral Address for Colin Carr
— given at St. James' Church, Grimsby, on September 20th, 2002
by the Rev. Canon Michael Hunter

"If it belongs to an artist not only to reflect life but to comment on it, then Colin Carr was a fine exponent of his craft. What better way to pour scorn on the vandalism of Grimsby's Market Square in the seventies than to paint innumerable pictures of how things once were, and could still have been. How ironic that on this, the day of Colin's funeral, we should see the re-birth of a Farmers' Market in the town centre.

"The unmeritorious aspirations of town planners and commercial developers were the constant focus of Colin Carr's wrath and frustration. One of my abiding memories of Colin was catching him taking photographs of the Wellowgate railway signal box on the day it disappeared from the landscape, and I swear I detected a tear in his eye.

"So this afternoon we come to join Ollie* (his wife) and the family in paying tribute to one of the town's great crusaders, an ambassador for a world of beauty and gracefulness, a hugely gifted artist and a friend who showed us that to be, at times, irritable, stubborn, difficult and eccentric, can be admirable qualities on a canvas of insipid indifference and blandness.

"No-one who visited Colin and Ollie in their ground floor flat could forget the experience. It was an educational tour of Grimsby's finest antiquarian museum — armorial porcelain, Chinese snuff boxes, blessing crosses and a selection of Royal Honours — all other people's alas! Photographs, letters, military memorabilia, a 1927 cricket cap, and a top hat belonging to the late Archdeacon Clifford Jarvis. Even Colin's best overcoat, which he wore on posh days at church, first saw the light of day in 1925.

"If his home reflected the man then so did his favourite haunts — Sandringham, Louth, Horncastle, Southwold and Cheltenham. And likewise his friends — Roy Faiers, Peter Chapman, Rolf Sperr, Wilf Bickley and many others whose creative flair matched his own. As Peter wrote so eloquently in the *Grimsby Telegraph* this week, we are all the poorer that Colin is no longer with us.

"Yet, of course, the joy of an artist is that his work, his message and his values live on. At the back of the church *This England's* calendar and the Colin Carr Christmas cards continue to be our best selling products in the church shop. I can testify that there are few houses I have visited in these parts which do not display a Colin Carr print or painting — or perhaps just a Christmas card framed because it was considered too valuable to discard with the rest. These are more than collectors' items, they are a joyous peep at a way of life and a happiness to which we all aspire.

"We are all in bereavement, and we wish to share the burden of sorrow and the loss felt by his wife and the family. There was not an occasion that I visited Colin in hospital, or at the nursing home, that I didn't find Ollie at his bedside.

So we come to salute the talent of a remarkable and a wonderful man. Behind the public artist was a warm, generous and vulnerable human being. This church will always be grateful to Colin, not just for including St. James' on so many of his paintings but because, year after year, he donated a painting for the prize draw at the Christmas Bazaar, raising hundreds of pounds for us at a time when it was desperately required.

"The characters in Colin's pictures were inevitably an expression of his own distinctiveness. We now pray that this man of great distinction will rest in peace and enjoy the same resurrection experience that he gave to so many of us."

*As this book was being prepared for press, we received the sad news that Colin's widow, Ollie, died suddenly, aged 71, barely four months after the loss of her husband. She had been a teacher at St. James' Church Choir School, Grimsby, for over 40 years and, as a Reader and regular participant in services at the parish church, was known as "Mother of the Choristers", many of whom came from all parts of Britain to attend her funeral service in February.

△St. James' Church and the Old Market, Grimsby, before developers began changing it.

Acknowledgements

We wish to acknowledge the helpful co-operation of family and friends of Colin Carr in the preparation of this book, including his widow, the late Mrs Olive Carr; brother Gordon, and sons Colin John and Christopher.

We also wish to thank Jean Lewis (sister-in-law); Canon Michael Hunter, Miss Merrilie Nicholson (Colin's teacher at Nunsthorpe School), Eileen Wallis, Anne Chidwick, Rolf Sperr, Peter Chapman of the *Grimsby Telegraph*; Judy Theobald of *Lincolnshire Life*, and Keren Bowers, Christine Manifold and Stephen Garnett of *This England*.